A Study of Banking and Professionalism and Ethics with consideration for Philosophy & Ethics theories

Michael AK

MCBI Chartered Banker GFSP CCBI

Photos from www.Pexels.com

ISBN: 978-1-917293-65-5

Chapter List

Regulation and causes of financial failure

One of the reasons that the financial sector is heavily regulated more than other sectors is the impact it has on people's lives and the effect on companies, without bank's modern civilization would crumble.

Another reason why the banks are heavily regulated is because of the diversity of services which are available in this modern age, and the innovation of banking services including online banking, telephone/mobile banking which has led to an increase in fraud which related to cybercrimes.

This includes fraud such as: banking credit card fraud, Ponzi and investment schemes.

The rise of cybercrime means stricter financial sector controls, this includes extra responsibilities from banking employees and tighter security checks such as handheld pin devices, facial recognition software, randomised unique number codes and password security.

Luigi Wegewege and Michael C. Thomsett, The Digital Banking revolution- How Fintech companies are transforming the retail banking industry through financial innovation 3rd Edition (2019, p 431) observes *"retail banks bundling services together with hidden charges and no need for central control"*.

A famous historical disaster in banking is Enron, mainly because of improper audit controls, uncontrolled risk and shareholder failure. Many of these previous historical events have led to tighter regulations, controls and extra responsibility from banking employees to avoid repeated history.

The features of banks which trigger bank employees to ensure that those products and services are right for the customer include: insurance services, wealth management, loans, credit card applications, and housing services.

This is because the customers can be harmed through improper usage and unwise decisions or lacking necessity. Banks will not entertain products unless the product or service is needed. This imposes extra responsibility on banking employees.

Ranald C. Michie, British banking continuity and change from 1694 to present (2016, p.33) observes " *Kindle Berger's account states its difficulty with government intervention led to customer abuse and unregulated banking areas*

Professionalisation is a transformative process in which a profession gains extra qualities. The idea of professionalism is linked to moral code, ethics and high standards.

Professionalisation can help banking employees to live up to their moral responsibilities through a strong sense of professionalism. Bankers are less likely to participate in unfair practices, since it would contradict the idea of professionalism. Furthermore, the business ethics code will prevent employees from committing immoral activities in financial or banking sectors.

For example, Mr Templeton is a chairman for Santander, he was recently offered a large cash sum in exchange for Santander client files and company data being sent to a competitor.

However, because Mr Templeton has been a banking professional for over 20 years, and has always followed the company code and ethics. He was not tempted by the offer and instead reported this incident to the necessary channels.

The Chartered Banker Code of Professional Conduct January (2016, p.3) observes " *principles of customer interest, fair treatment and market conduct, acting with honesty and trust also avoiding clash of duty and personal interest scenarios* ".

3

Lawyers, Doctors, Solicitors, Architects and Athletes would be considered professionals, these group of individuals carry out different functions within society. Similarly, the code helps bankers with professionalization because of the values in the code and helps a banker to maintain their moral responsibilities.

Knowledge and devotion to these values enable a banker or any professional employee to live up to their moral responsibilities.

The idea of professionalisation is companies maintaining highly professional standards without constant sanctions by regulatory firms. Since a company ignoring these standards would receive negative spotlight, lose status and receive harsh sanctions. Understanding the balancing of principles and notions of autonomy and moral obligation, helps bank employees live up to their moral responsibilities.

Justine Rogers, Dimity Kingsford Smith and John Chellew -Banking and the Limits of Professionalism (2017, p.4) observes: *"consideration of banking features applicable to professionalising leads to sociological questions on professionalising qualities and principles"*

If the code of professional conduct were rewritten, principle one will include that respect and acting with integrity encompasses all banking activities and the banker's professional career, including both ethical and moral action.

However, principle two on maintaining professional knowledge and acting with care and diligence, when considering the risks and implications of actions and advice is praiseworthy. This is because it can be applied to many professions. This can be likened to universalizability, whereby there is a maxim which all individuals can act on within a similar circumstance.

ICAEW Jim Baxter, James Dempsey, Chris Megone and Jongseok Lee- Real Integrity Practical Solutions for Organisations Seeking to Encourage Integrity (2012, p4) observes "*integrity is crucial to the codes and professional firm ideologies encourage ethical thoughts and patterns from their members*".

Therefore, the inclusion of integrity as the number one precept in the Chartered Banker code of conduct is a key concept.

It should be worth mentioning the institute and faculty of actuaries' code, which has six principles and is similar to the Chartered Banker code. It improves upon some of the terms which are mentioned in the Chartered banker code of conduct.

Principle three regarding being open and cooperative with the regulators and complying with all current regulatory principles, this needs to ensure that practices and activities are always legal and that there is virtue in compliance. It can be likened to Aristotle's virtue.

Robert E. Frederick- A companion to business Ethics (1999, p.30) observes "*in his Niomachean Ethics, Aristotle laid the groundwork for virtue ethics and was regarded as the pioneer, setting the framework or standard for virtue ethics. Virtue meant leaning on the further side of moderation in a Greek sense*"

5

Principle four should have the addition of fairness including equality and being honest as a banker and professional.

When observing and demonstrating proper standards of market conduct at all times, it is important that you remain impartial whilst observing proper standards of conduct, and behaving with integrity whilst observing these standard. The reason why this is important is because of bad business practices and individuals interested in maximising profit or selling products which do not suit the needs of the customer(mis-selling).

Principle seven denotes sensitive and confidential data. This principle needs consideration for storage, disposal, monitoring sensitive and confidential financial data for security purposes.

Aristotle's concept of virtue is considered as one of the ethical requirements, which as mentioned above can be related to the Chartered Banker's code of conduct.

Linda K. Trevino, Katherine A. Nelson Managing Business Ethics- straight talk about how to do it right ,6th edition (2014, p.348)observes *"ethical responsibilities, legal responsibilities, a tobacco company taking responsibility for the harmful advert aimed at minors"*

An example of a banking practice which is legal and unethical is the selling of policies to customers who obtained loans, with high premium and rates with insurance quality that was subpar. In this example selling these products breaches the banker's code of conduct.

An example of illegal banking practices include: high street banks or credit companies collecting unauthorised money, breaking laws which protect the consumer for profit. Some lenders give expensive insurance and take funds from providers.

One other example of illegal business practice is the inclusion of expensive closing and ending fees due to illegal contracts.

Linda K. Trevino, Katherine A. Nelson Managing Business Ethics- straight talk about how to do it right 6th edition (2014, p.348)observes *"business laws are crucial principles of the business system and running parallel to financial responsibilities, legality is considered the least values and ideals of enterprise behaviour confirmed by civilization.*

Ethical Theories and Criticisms of Ethical Theories

One of the ethical theories which I have chosen is deontology which may sometimes become known as Kantianism. Kant states that good will was essentially a form of the highest good.

Acting with good will and acting within duty, Kant focused on the action's maxim.

R.G Frey and Christopher Heath Wellman - A companion to Applied Ethics (p.30,2005): states *"Deontological theories depart from consequentialism on this fundamental point, purely concerned with action and not outcome"*

The intent is what makes the act good, the main criticism of deontology is the school of teleological arguments. Which states that you must be concerned with the end result of the action or effect. Kant was concerned with the intent of the act and not the consequences of the act.

Ethical relativism is the second ethical theory, there are customs which are diverse in other cultures, and the claim of ethical relativism is that due to the different values of morality within cultures there are therefore no norms which can be overlapped or applied broadly.

Robert E.Frederick- A companion to business Ethics (1999, p.69) observes *"EA alternative, ER explores moral diversity with moral reference"*

The key criticism of ethical relativism is that because everything is relative it is difficult to measure scale, and morality may be considered relative.

The final theory is consequentialism which is a terminology given to a set of ethical theories, concerned with the consequences of an action. When given a moral problem, this branch looks at obtaining the consequence which is best.

The consequentialist is concerned with the bad or harm which occurs from the consequences, also the calculation of harms.

R.G Frey and Christopher Heath Wellman - A companion to Applied Ethics (p.26,2005): observes *"consequentialism explores norms held before morality, actions are still evil or good without right or wrong"*

The criticism of consequentialism is the school of deontology, consequentialism is not concerned with bad moral acts or ill intended acts provided the consequence is positive.

All of these theories can be used to criticize one and other, deontology can criticize ethical relativism, consequentialism can criticize deontology and consequentialism can be criticized by deontology. The important point is to understand the importance of all theories and possibly even create a new school of thought or theory, when evaluating or criticizing.

A potential dispute regarding staff member A giving out personal client data to a competitor or another bank such as: HSBC. Another staff member B found out and was arguing with staff member A about how unethical the act was.

The consequence-based strategy which individual A adopts is that the data will also be used, for business purposes and once the business has been concluded the data will be destroyed. There will not be significant harm done to the current company or client, the client will benefit from two bank services.

Linda K. Trevino, Katherine A. Nelson Managing Business Ethics- straight talk about how to do it right 6th edition (2014,p.40) observes *"theories considered consequentialist, focus on the end and reason, concerned with the moral right or wrong outcomes or resulting actions".*

However, staff member B would adopt the strategy from a deontological aspect, looking at the action as opposed to having concern with the consequence. The more specific definition would be concern over the morality of an action, the morals would be whether the action is good, bad, pure or evil.

Linda K. Trevino, Katherine A. Nelson Managing Business Ethics- straight talk about how to do it right 6th edition (2014, p.42) observes *"deontological theories are concerned with duty. They consider the duty of the action regarding consequences".*

In the eyes of staff member B this action is abhorrent, since this action breaches the data protection act, it also infringes on the individual's privacy and human rights. This makes the strategy invalid and not sound for staff member B, since it breaks ethical and legal responsibilities.

The strategy which staff member A has adopted, the consequentialist strategy has merit, the consequence of giving the data to another bank or competitor will benefit the customer. It could be a valid argument that the customer could get better advice or service from the other bank, however this is one positive outcome. The negative aspects are the infringement of ethical and legal rights, human rights and the breach of GDPR.

There is no consideration for whether the individual wants the services provided by the other bank, this action is intrusive and also affects the privacy of the individual, the soundness of the argument cannot be questioned, the failings of the strategy are ethical, moral and legal failings. This strategy fails the validity test, which is whether it can be reasoned with logic or fact. The logic is flawed since the customer loses personal data and the facts are not positive.

The strategy adopted by staff member B is relatively sound, because the actions prevent a potential data breach, whilst maintaining integrity and moral code.

However, consideration should be given to the potential conflict or whistleblowing scenario.

The actions of staff member B could be seen as being socially responsible for his or her own actions within the business. This could lead to the business gaining a better reputation or face by appearing more socially aware.

When working for a private hire company, there was a time when a customer insulted a fellow worker. The employee was considering retaliating by cancelling their account and revoking premium status, this act is not virtuous and breaks Aristotle's concept of virtue. This behaviour was challenged using ethical reasoning and theories.

Ethical principles are guidelines for these types of situations, the ethical reasoning is that cancelling and revoking the customer's premium status, causes doubt on the employee's ethical persuasion and the private hire business. It is important to act with integrity, honesty and respect as a business professional.

Ethical reasoning and business decision making state that these unethical business decisions have monetary value or cost. Ethical principles reach a conclusion or consensus when faced with these ethical problems. The failure of the employee to understand unethical acts, and issues. Whilst not considering another perspective or opposing viewpoint of the issue or decisions which need to be considered is failed ethical reasoning. This was something which was explained.

Many ethical theories state that an organisation should be based on solid ethical rules. The fellow employee would be breaking solid ethical rules by taking actions against the customer.

Robert E.Frederick- A companion to business Ethics it is observed (1999, p.150) *"Blanchard and Peale (1988) - managers question on decision making, should consider legality, balance and situational feelings about the action"*.

Another example of when a hypothetical individual at work wished to do something was when I was involved in dealing with the process of the contracts for due diligence. There was a hypothetical individual that wished to skip some of the legal procedures including the financial check, which is performed to determine whether the organisation has a good score to register their contract.

This potentially leads to a company being registered on a contract which was not entirely legal, this behaviour was challenged using ethical reasoning. The reasoning which was used was whether the individual's actions are legal. Was the action balanced and when considering the wrongness of the act and negative consequences, the emotions which are evoked?

Furthermore, the employee should always consider whether the action will lead to a good outcome regardless of the situation or circumstances.

ICAEW Jim Baxter, James Dempsey, Chris Megone, Jongseok Lee- Real Integrity Practical Solutions for Organisations Seeking to Encourage Integrity (2012) states *Integrity is a much-desired but little understood feature of organisations and of the individuals they employ.*

14

Legislation and Acts or Regulations affecting the Financial Industry

The Financial Service Markets Act 2000 is a parliamentary act that created the financial services authority, the financial services authority are responsible for regulation in the investment and banking sector. Regulation is ubiquitous in the financial sector, therefore it will have a large impact on customers, employees and everybody.

There are the markets in financial instruments directive, MifiD II and MIFIR replaces the previous version MIFIR known as the pillar of the EU financial law. This directive deals with investment activities licencing services and decisions. This has a large impact on the customers dealing with investment and the employees must adhere to these regulations

There is also the market abuse regulation, this regulation was introduced in July 2016, looks at providing increased market integrity, protection for investors and raising of capital for securities markets. Mar applies to financial instruments related to instruments traded on a market regulated for admission request for market trading, This affects customers and banking employees, as well as business investors and has a large impact.

There is also the Bank of England (Amendment) (EU Exit) Regulations 2018 which includes provisions on UK legislation which would facilitate Brexit. Brexit will affect all individuals and many sectors including the financial sector, the impact of these regulations will affect the way in which banks carry out business.

Another piece of legislation is the introduction of the fifth money laundering directive which essentially improves and overhauls the fourth money laundering directive. This increases the scope and now encompasses virtual currency providers, which deal in exchanges of fiat currency and virtual currency and associated services. This affects the customers and individuals involved in virtual currency mainly fiat currency. There is little impact for other individuals since they don't trade in fiat currency.

There is also the Senior Managers and Certification Regime, the aim is to increase the responsibility and accountability of senior managers, it changes the framework which governs the financial service sector. This has no impact on customers or individuals not directly involved in the financial sector. It will help banking employees to feel empowered.

Banks are regulated in order to prevent the failure of the banking system and banks as individuals and also to maintain confidence, integrity and trust in banks.

The laws and regulations in banking are mainly designed to act as controls for banks and to ensure the customers feel assured, when doing business with their bank.

When thinking of significant banking failure, it is important to remember the case of Enron, which was a catastrophic banking disaster and reduced trust and confidence in banks.

The reason for banking failure can be attributed to inefficient decisions regarding investments, the banks are unable to accommodate the speed of customer withdrawals, over time it leads to a deficit. This erodes trust and confidence in banks since customers feel a lack of service.

Ranald C. Michie, British banking continuity and change from 1694 to present (2016, p.185-p.186) observes *"in 1986, lack of regulation, resulted in mass expansion of banks, fusing retail and investment in banking, Barclays fused investment services with securities services. This fusion was unsuccessful"*.

However too much regulation means high government control, this could cause banks to have reduced services, increased barriers to entry, increased secure asset culture, increased regulator input such as FCA, bank of England, stricter international banking regulation, financial service co-ordination and tighter liquidation regulations. This decreases trust and confidence in banks, because banking ability is too heavily restricted and regulated, banking users are adversely affected.

Ranald C. Michie, British banking continuity and change from 1694 to present (2016, p.33) observes *"Kindleberger's classic account states it was difficult for governments to balance intervening in the banking system. This drove financial activity into completely unregulated areas little government regulation, left banking service users open to abuse and led to risks"*.

This warns of the dangers of de-regulation, customers were vulnerable and open to market abuse. There was accumulated financial risk as well, de-regulation meant reduced governmental control, increased market competition, market freedom which is beneficial for banks. However de-regulation also means re-allocation of resources. There was also an increase in bad business

17

practices including: bogus loans, unwanted contract terms and financial deals, this affects the reputation of banks since there is reduced trust and confidence in the service.

The arguments for banking regulation are tighter and stricter controls, less chances of fraud, less chances of bogus loans and financial offers, this will in turn help banks and bankers to maintain standards and act in a lawful and ethical manner, regulation ensures trade within the financial sector is fair, the maintenance of fair competition and "free" market values under regulation.

Within the banking industry if the culture is not target driven and heavily regulated, this could lead to a reduction in poor ethical practices such as: deceiving customers, unwanted products and fees and dangerous financial schemes. This would rebuild trust and confidence in banks since customers would feel safe and secure.

The argument for de-regulation is increased banking activity and competition, larger availability of services, increased financial flexibility, merging of financial services, potential creation of a universal bank, reduced barriers to entry, increased low price products etc.

In conclusion the main reason for regulation is because of public security and a customer orientated outlook. This is related to the code of conduct, the idea of banks and organisations being socially responsible and aware of their short comings and negatives. But mostly the reason why de-regulation cannot work is related to public security issues and public finances. If there was a large-scale de-regulation it would lead to customers receiving unfair practices, it may also lead to similar disaster on the scale of Enron. De-regulation would require a leap of faith in trust and confidence which history has not proved to be successful.

Social Responsibility and Corporate Social Responsibility with theories

Social responsibility for business was described by Milton Friedman as using resources to participate in activities which give increased profit, observing rules in open and free competition, no fraud or deceptive elements with lawfulness and moral values.

The quotation from R.G Frey and Christopher Heath Wellman- A companion to Applied Ethics (2003, p.538) observes *"one principle, social responsibility using company power to increase profits whilst indulging in open and free competition and discouraging fraudulent or deceitful business practices (Friedman,1970:126)"*

Friedman is arguing that management owes a duty to shareholders or owners. Milton is also referring to sharing company profits, dividends, shareholder, ROI and ethical company practices. Friedman in another quote also includes meeting other ends and goals.

Linda K. Trevino, Katherine A. Nelson Managing Business Ethics- straight talk about how to do it right 6th edition (2014, p348) observes *"Friedman states the sole responsibility is shareholder profit maximization. However also to make a large money sum, under society ethical and lawful values or principles".*

Milton Friedman wants to maximise the profits of the shareholders and investors, whilst conforming to society's norms.

There was a case of where Volkswagen created a design which skirted emissions control and gave them a huge lead over their competitors in car manufacturing. The story was that these cars were environmentally friendly when the opposite was actually true. Volkswagen are not operating under Milton's societal, ethical and lawful values or principle due to deception and legal failure.

The team rejected any form of ethical standard test which would have highlighted the issues on corporate social responsibility. The legal obligation is providing a product which is correctly displayed. This would be a case of the buyer being wary of this product. They have gone beyond the legal and ethical implications which Milton states are a part of social responsibility.

The processes, software, equipment and results were all on record, it is clear that Volkswagen deliberately hid the fact that this motor was not environmentally friendly, this leads back to the concept of virtue, integrity and even Milton Friedman's concept of responsibility. They were more interested in the maximisation of profit as opposed to environmental, factors, green energy and CSR.

It could however be argued that if Milton Friedman were a shareholder, that Volkswagen have used resources and activities to increase profit, they have also increased profit within the confines of the game or market.

The company may convince Milton Friedman that this is not fraud or deception, but simply an error in the checking and testing processes.

Linda K. Trevino, Katherine A. Nelson Managing Business Ethics- straight talk about how to do it right 5th edition (2010, p330)   *-The statement also means that some businesses should not exist because society has deemed them to be harmful no matter what their potential for profit*

They may present the claim to Milton that they are unaware of any ethical or legal principles which they are breaking, all of the equipment and testing was present and guidelines were followed.

The team would argue that Milton Friedman who believed in free competition in the market sector, should encourage their efforts to become market leaders through advertising a product. Which supposedly embodies CSR which Milton supports. Volkswagen would argue that they produce the highest standard of product.

Another argument which can be adopted is that since Milton Friedman believed the government to be a monstrosity, it could be said that the companies attempt to obtain a larger market share and create a monopoly, does not resort in economies of scale for the government.

A company may fail to justify its policies to Milton Friedman, for instance if Barclays bank decided to implement a policy that ignored shareholders duty, they may fail to justify shareholder profit maximization being too costly because of the ROI or capital which needs to be returned and is not worth it.

Barclays bank may fail to justify using older banking technology with known bugs and firmware or data issues, they may argue that using older technology and hiding this fact is less costly than obtaining new technology which has better functions and security. They may fail to justify the need for deception in business to Milton.

Barclays bank may decide to deny social responsibility and individualism. They may opt for products and services which deny individual responsibility and the family and instead present a focus on technology. They may fail to justify that implementing products which have individualism or family themes is too costly.

Barclays bank may fail to justify to Milton that ideas on individual freedom are naïve and costly in the business world, they may argue that the concept of freedom is relative from employee to employee. Barclays may argue that an implementation of a free philosophy in the workplace would be costly due to individual needs, it will erode current banking regulations or legal principles, and freedom is not the ultimate value.

Alexander Brink- Corporate Governance and Business Ethics (2011, p.194) states that *"Market and the price of shares form the basis of corporate performance notifications and are not biased.this represents shareholder mentality" (cf. Keynes 1936; Shiller 1989)"*

Barclays may state that with regards to Milton's statement on freedom to make mistakes, as a competitive market leader it is important the business is seen a company that is almost perfect, there is also a business cost for mistakes. Barclays may fail to justify this fact to Milton on the basis that the financial sector history is filled with mistakes.

Adopting a Keynesian approach involves government expenditure whereas Milton is only concerned with the control of money, the banks would argue that shareholder duty is overtaken by expenditure, the argument is that money is not the only justification and the economy is not quickly affected by this.

The Keynesian approach looks more closely at aggregate demand, they would argue that selling of products and services aimed at the individual or family is too simplistic when considering market demand.

Keynesians who argue about the importance of government expenditure and low taxes would state the presence of individualism and freedom in business or the market erodes government expenditure. There needs to be more spending on public services including education to increase this expenditure and freedom does not directly increase this.

Keynesians would also state that company mistakes reduce consumer demand, due to negative market reputation and this has an adverse effect on the market.

In conclusion whilst, Milton Friedman's policy is idealistic, it does not take account of every market variable. Milton ignores aggregate demand and government expenditure. He also prioritizes shareholder interest. However, Milton would be correct in this argument in this example since Barclays is breaking both legal and ethical principles.

Leadership

Jacqueline Boakes questions whether leadership must not be democratic, her conclusion looks at the meaning of the relationship between both democracy and leadership. Leadership in regards to democracy may be considered agnostic or neutral. Certain types of leadership have higher rates of compatibility than other types with regards to democracy. This is due to the fact that we have reasons, which are not associated with democracy but which allow us to value it. Leadership is not compatible with democracy because of its intrinsic nature, some leadership styles support the way of democracy and its values. Concerning leadership with democracy there are attributes of leadership which are compatible with democracy, the true understanding of leadership will bind successfully with democracy. The extent to what makes a good leader is based on the leadership style being compatible with democracy. There is no consideration for ethics or good morals of the leader.

Jacqueline Boaks & Michael P Levine-Leadership & Ethics (2015, p.8) states *"Kouzes (2010: xvii) assumption of knowledge of participants regarding leadership qualities, unconvincing responses do not follow cited evidence.*

The Ethics of authentic leadership by Jessica Flannigan, states that authenticity is supported because of its positive moral attributes for leaders

Inauthenticity may be likened with wrongful or deceitful acts such as deceiving an individual or acting as a hypocrite, the balance of decision for authenticity is related to an emphasis on equal morals. Most inauthentic leaders, usually do not give their followers the chance to agree to the plan of the leader and they do not acknowledge these individuals as equal individuals with rights to equal morality. However authentic leaders have loyalty which does not have illusions and has occurred in a just way with clear consent of their followers, leaders which are not authentic blame their followers and deny their equal moral rights by holding them to higher standards. An inauthentic leader may be altruistic in his intentions, a lack of authenticity is considered wrong because it lacks respect. It may be justifiable, in most cases it stems from mistaken morality permissible when it has not risen to the level of deception. There is some consideration for the good moral actions of leaders. The extent of good leadership is based on authenticity, loyalty and moral actions or standard.

Kant focuses on the intention behind the action as opposed to the action itself which one should be concerned with. There is no consideration for this in either theory.

In Robert E.Frederick- A companion to business Ethics (1999,p.4) it is stated *"Kantian morals, distinguishing between two duty definitions, what is duty according to Kant"*

In conclusion, whilst I agree with concept from both theories regarding authenticity and democracy. I would support Jessica Flannigan's view of the leader because it explores the leader's actions. However, I believe that her theory could be improved with the idea of the philosopher king. Social, political, ethical and ultimately metaphysical attributes can be given to the idea behind Plato's philosopher king as a style of leadership, Plato gives the example that the most suited leader exerts the most fear and achieve true leadership.

Some of the technological developments include online banking and money transfer. There is also a new fraud detection system. These systems make banking practices more ethical through increased customer safety.

Other technological developments include telephone banking which allows an individual to acccss their banking services such transfers, direct debit and checking of balance by inputting their card number into the phone, and going through security questions and inputting sensitive information.

UK Finance Ethical use of customer data in a digital economy (2019, p.10) observes *"the usage and broad applications of AI algorithms and the necessary flexibility in dealing with this technology area"*

Looking at this statement from an ethical standpoint, it is clear that the usage of technology has brought a range of issues which touch on corporate social responsibility, ethical implications and legal implications.

The legal responsibilities would form the norms required by society for business to follow, responsibilities include code of conduct, contracts, banking regulations, banking employee legal rights, terms and conditions of loans etc.

The ethical responsibilities are another layer beyond the legal requirements, looking at how an individual is endangered by ethical company actions, exploring unethical business practices. Companies adopt legal loopholes to commit unethical acts including: modern slavery, sweatshop workers, bogus work contracts and human trafficking.

The consideration for environmental factors relates to dealing with the issue related to climate change and the attempt to reduce our carbon foot print through an economy promoting low carbon usage.

It may be argued that another environmental factor is recession, recession means businesses and banks must lower costs and overheads etc. Another factor which may be considered is the repayments associated with loans. These factors can lead to unethical and bad business practices including unscrupulous loans, bad contracts, unwanted banking products and mis selling.

The issue is that all of the factors which lead to economic growth provide a direct increase in CO_2 emissions which causes pollution, climate change and global warming. Corporate social responsibility states that the organisation is responsible socially for its produce and investors and stakeholders.

Alexander Brink- Corporate Governance and Business Ethics (2011, p.250) observes *"CSR is widespread in the US, more than 80% of executives confirm CSR is crucial to businesses"*

The argument for banks having a moral obligation towards the environment, one of the ideas which would support this argument is the idea of corporate social responsibility, this theory states companies should be aware of their responsibility to appear as organisations. Which acknowledge and address their shortcomings and also look to always have socials awareness and political understanding of their company's position and undertakings.

Ideas such as: having green energy and considering the effect of waste and business practices on the environment, a simple example would be a bank using paper-based storage which is not environmentally friendly and does not align with CSR.

The features of banks include insurance services, checking accounts, savings accounts, wealth management, loans, ISA, debit and credit cards, merchant services, personal banking, business banking, online banking, telephone banking, mobile check deposit boxes, tablet banking, text alerts, statements, personal loans, equity loans, home equity lines of credit, home loans, business loans.

There are many organisations which regulate the financial sector, there is the financial industry regulatory board, there is also the FCA, the FCA are the regulator for over 50,000 financial firms, financial markets in the UK and over 16,000 of those firm's prudential regulator.

The goal is that the financial market is an honest, fair-trading place where consumers can obtain services in open and free competition, this goes from big companies, small business, individuals and investors, as a prudential regulator it is necessary that customers are aware that the firms they do business with are safe, sound and honest.

One of the reasons that financial sector is heavily regulated more than other sectors is the impact which the sector has on people's lives and the effect on companies, without banks modern civilization would crumble there would be a difficulty with establishing trade and currency would become meaningless without a means to store and trade on it.

Another reason why the banks are heavily regulated is because of the diversity of services which are available in this modern age, the innovation of banking services including online banking, telephone/ mobile banking has led to an increase in types of fraud which are related to cybercrimes.

This includes simple fraud such as 419 and other schemes, it can also be an individual posing as a director and obtaining funds from your bank account or even a person sending an email which could compromise your system and allow them to obtain personal/ bank account data, there is even the possibility of the individual creating a server which will hide their location, while they hack your server or send malware or emails which allow to them compromise your system.

The rise of cybercrime has led to more stricter controls for the financial sector, this includes tighter security checks such as handheld pin devices, facial recognition software, long number code which is randomized, the use of passwords and confirmation of an individual's date of birth.

in previous times, German banks would opt to have reduced risk and an iron clad relationship when dealing with corporations and they would give an investment and have no expectation of a return of capital, recent practices of banking look at reducing the risk and client asset diversification whilst maintaining long distance relations with their client

a famous historical disaster in banking is Enron, which occurred due to uncontrolled risk and no controls in place to mitigate the risk, also both shareholders /creditors were deceived.

When considering the disaster of Enron, it is prudent to consider the previous dates inlcuding:1974, 1914, 1866, 1878 and 1890, since they may be considered in a similar bracket, whilst these may be looked upon a separate incident in banking which were perhaps minor crises, these dates can be considered as small disruptions or preludes that affect British banking stability.

The crisis which occurred in 2007 and 2008 created a stir in the history and may be marked in the history of British banking, it was considered vastly different form the crisis which had occurred in the past, it was however concluded that this has happened beforehand on several occasions.

Many of these previous historical events have led to tighter regulations and controls within the banking sector in order to avoid repeated disaster.

A strong ideal of professionalism and having a code which is related to ethics can help banking employees live up to their moral responsibilities, because by having strong sense of professionalism they are less likely to participate in unfair practices because this is not what a professional would do, furthermore the ethical code of business which they follow will prevent them from committing immoral activities in the financial or banking sector.

For example, Mr Leon who has been working as a chairman for Santander was recently offered a large sum of money in order to give some Santander client files and company data to a competitor.

However, because Mr Leon has been a banking professional for over 20 years and has always followed the code of ethics, he was not even tempted by this proposition and instead reported this incident to the necessary channels.

The concept of professionalization of bankers must be defined, it is important to mention the code of conduct for chartered bankers which mentions treating customers fairly and acting with integrity, the mention of integrity is an important value for bankers, if I have integrity, this means that I have a strong moral compass and I always act in a way which is honest.

These are the qualities of a banker, it is also important to note that professionalism in the financial industry is competing with commercialism.

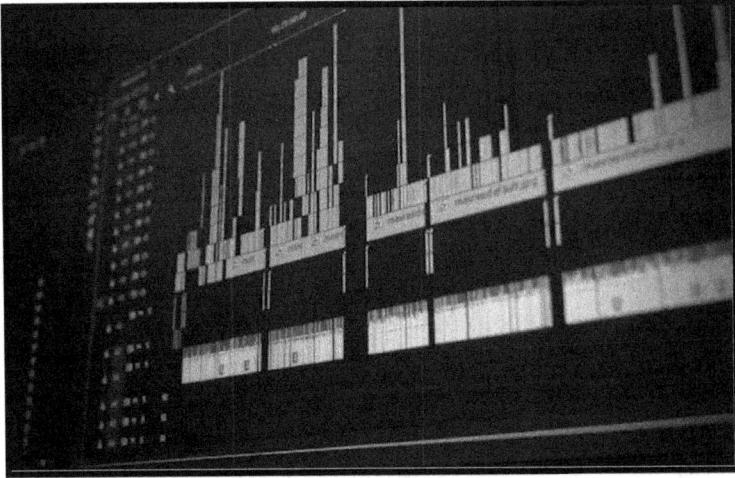

The banking standards board was designed to encourage standards which were high and to promote a high level of competency, this also includes the matter of regulation and professionalization.

Part of the regulation has included setting up a framework which can compensate for the high regulatory needs of banking, the idea behind professionalisation is that your company or organisation maintain these high standards without the constant need to be sanctioned by other regulatory firms.

This ensures that firms maintain standards which are highly professional, if they did not maintain these standards, it would be obvious to many within the market and their company would lose status and eventually receive harsh sanctions.

The view of professionalization in professional bodies is that it is a positive step, it encourages cohesion and helps with controlling quality and could lead to a better relationship for firms, regulators and professional bodies.

An example of banking practice is that was legal but not ethical is the selling of policies to customers who obtained loans, with high premium and rates and the quality of the insurance was subpar.

The banks were interested in maximising returns and profits over a short-term period.

An example of illegal banking practices is high street banks or credit companies collecting money which was not theirs to earn, going against the laws which protect the consumer in order to obtain more funds and lenders may provide expensive insurance and take a cut from the providers, there may also be expensive ending or closing fees due illegal tenets within the contracts.

Whilst you may argue that having insurance is ethically beneficial when looking at the principles and morality of insurance, however because in this case it has been done in a way to extort the consumer and using illegal means it can barely be considered ethical.

in previous times, German banks would opt to have reduced risk and an iron clad relationship when dealing with corporations and they would give an investment and have no expectation of a return of capital, recent practices of banking look at reducing the risk and client asset diversification whilst maintaining long distance relations with their client

Professionalism and Code Of Conduct

If I were to re write the code of professional conduct, I would write that treating all customers, colleagues and counterparties with respect and acting with integrity encompasses all of your banking activities and professional career, it should also include acting with a way which is both ethical and moral whilst fulfilling the personal commitment to the banking profession.

I would rewrite the development and maintaining my professional knowledge and acting with skill, care and diligence, considering the risks and implications of my actions and advice and holding myself accountable for them and their impact, I would rewrite this paragraph to include the mention of full accountability and that as a chartered banker it is important to remain impartial and objective when providing advice and carrying out actions.

I would rewrite that whilst being open and cooperative with the regulators and complying with all current regulatory and legal requirements, it is important to ensure that practices and activities are always legal and that you are also virtuous in your compliance. It may be worth simply mentioning Aristotle's meaning of virtue which may be used as a reference for the code.

Robert E.Frederick- A companion to business Ethics states *"in his Niomachean Ethics, Aristotle laid out the system for virtue ethics which still remains the starting point, if not the model for most virtue ethicists A virtue for Aristotle was the mean between the extremes something more than the usual Greek emphasis on moderation."*

I would rewrite that it is important to pay due regard to the interests of customers and treating them fairly, the concept of fairness should also include equality and being honest as a banker and professional.

I would rewrite observing and demonstrating proper standards of market conduct at all times, it is important that you remain impartial whilst observing proper standards of conduct, and that you behave in a way which demonstrated values of integrity when demonstrating these standards.

I would rewrite that it is imperative to act in an honest and trustworthy manner, being alert to and managing potential conflicts of interest; and treating information with appropriate confidentiality and sensitivity in your role in banking, it is also important that adopt a professional approach when managing conflicts of interest and that there is no element of nepotism, also with regards to sensitive and confidential data it is important to consider how you store, dispose and monitor sensitive and confidential financial data as an individual within the banking profession.

I would rewrite the part regarding developing and maintaining professional knowledge and acting with skills care and diligence when considering risks, I would change this point to include the need to adapt to all situations when considering risks and it is also important to use professional knowledge with the usage of situational judgement, this means that you should always consider different scenarios and variables when applying professional knowledge.

Treating information with appropriate confidentiality and sensitivity, this should include some of the data protection act precepts and the need to label data or group data according to the scale of sensitivity.

The financial sector is heavily regulated and this raises unique ethical issues, regulation is based upon traditional values including fairness and the fiduciaries role, the financial market is plagued by unfair practices, fraud is large and diverse in the sector and has a leading and diverse role. Fair trade, open and structured competition should be the picture of the financial market, including terms of trade being made on level surfaces, efficiency and fairness are needed for ethical profit maximisation, there needs to be security even for federal legal bodies and regulation which intermediaries or financial companies may undertake.

Bogus contracts, unusual terms and underhand practices can occur from manipulation, incorrect enforcement and interpretation causing bad experiences for consumers and professionals.

Aristotle's concept of virtue is one of the ethical requirements required of a banker, a person who acts in a way which is virtuous, this could be described as courageous or even being able to objectively view actions within the bank and act as a professional when dealing with a difficult or rude customer may be considered virtuous since it requires courage

There are various concepts which could be looked at when considering ethics in banking/ finance, it is important to behave with integrity, to be seen to be respectable, open/ transparent in your dealings and to be seen as fair.

This can be related to the chartered bankers code of conduct which mentions treating all customers with fairness and considering the customers interests with fairness.

Furthermore, it can be observed that having a bank or financial institute which is ethical and has solid ethical values. This makes the organisation trusted and they will appear more honest. Since in order to be ethical an individual or organisation must consider the intentions and morality of their actions. The ethics are a guideline which will keep the organisation on a straight moral compass. It can also affect the organisation's structure, work culture and approach.

Strategy and policy are dictated by company culture and related to the business's ethical stance, the FCA as regulators wish to appear impartial and objective, they have decided that company culture is flexible.

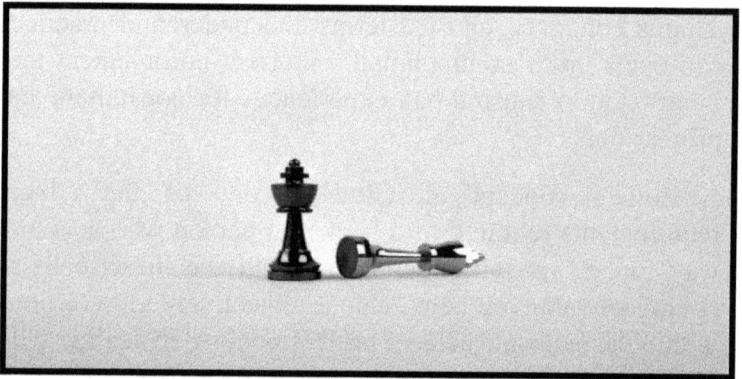

Company sustainability has little correlation with business ethics, an important factor to consider is the business model made up of stakeholders, shareholders consumers and the effect of organization's environment on this,

The lawmakers and regulators do not dictate what a business does, instead codes of conduct, guidelines and precepts are given to follow, following these principles will satisfy the bare minimum and maintain a standard framework for customers and shareholders.

The financial regulators are the financial conduct authority, prudential regulation authority and bank of England.

The controls which an organisation may have in place could be linked to auditing, a mechanism which prevents the company from going in the red or being forced to commit bad ethical decisions,

Staff are comprised of juniors, middle managers, senior management directors, chief of Board or chief of staff/Executive level.

Finally, the Banking Act 2009 is a piece of legislation which allows the PRA, FCA and BOE with the authority and ammunition to protect the financial stability of the country, by resolving failing banks and protecting depositors etc.

This act sets out the legal requirements of banks which affects bankers such as to ensure the continuity of critical banking functions and banking services, protection and enhancement of the UK's financial system in regard s to stability, increase public confidence in the stability of the system and protect and enhance this.

Recap of Kant and exploration of Corporate Social Responsibility/other theories including Plato and Global warming

Kant states the need to treat individuals as an end and not as a means, taking action on principles which can be made into universal precepts, acting as an individual of a kingdom which held ideals concerned with ends and you are both the ruler and the subject of this kingdom.

However, when considering the teleological aspect, it is important to note that consequence of shutting down services temporarily has resulted in the banking service working perfectly the next day. This in effect meant that more people were able to conduct their business the next day and an issue was avoided because of this single calculated decision.

Therefore, as is typical of deontological arguments, Kant was concerned with the intent of the act and not the consequences of the act.

The intent is what makes the act good, the main criticism of deontology is the school of teleological arguments which state that you must be concerned with the end result of the action or effect and not consideration for action or the intent.

The level of corruption within governments and the existence of this corruption is universal, in other words it exists everywhere, the Human Rights Act is ever changing to become more comprehensive however the basic human rights would not generally be considered a relative concept although there may be variations on the exact definition and the degrees which it includes

Another concept which may be challenged for relativism is the concept of justice, an example of a misuses of justice exists within countless examples of history such as; the crusades and some legal cases.

Is there a general meaning of justice or is this just simply assumed and applied to different levels and situations, the key criticism of ethical relativism is that because everything is relative it is difficult to measure things on a scale, morality may be considered relative and the same may be said for bad or evil acts. Whilst it can be argued that even with the lack of norms which overlap in cultures, there can still be acts which are considered inhumane, intrinsically bad or evil. This would include cannibalism, trafficking and killing.

It can also be considered a consequentialist because it looks at the teleological aspect of the argument which is whether the action produces a good or bad result or consequence, the concept of utility is argued by many philosophers some believe that the highest pursuit of utility lies in the form of hedonistic values or pleasure, since utility is has such a relative meaning this makes this branch difficult to define definitively

The utilitarian concept is concerned with obtaining the best consequence or best outcome, The phrase which sums it up is having the best outcome or consequence which benefits the most people or the greater good.

It is a concept of utility, therefore, it is unconcerned with the act itself and more concerned with whether the consequence has achieved a favourable result for many individuals, this is both a strength and huge criticism of this theory.

R.G Frey and Christopher Heath Wellman 2005- A companion to Applied Ethics *states" consequentialism begins with values it holds to be prior to morality, even if there were no moral right or wrong some things would still be good and others. "*

The criticism of consequentialism is the school of deontology, consequentialism is unconcerned with morally bad acts or ill intended acts provided the consequence is positive and morally good or achieves the greater good. A simple example of the problem with this theory, would be if there was an individual in the bank who decided to rob the bank with an armed gang. However, the robber was robbing the bank in order to use the money to save the lives of individuals in an orphanage, according to consequentialism this may be considered a good situation because the individual is committing a bad act in order to save the lives of many and whilst there is the potential to harm those at the bank, the end result is that the money used benefits the greater good. This theory unfortunately allows the justification of wicked or unethical acts to satisfy the greater good, result or a favourable consequence. It would allow a banker to sacrifice their integrity or duty for the sake of saving the members of the company or the public.

Within the banking industry there can be a target driven or orientated culture,

This could lead to poor ethical practices such as: deceiving customers with bogus accounts, exorbitant, unwanted fees and products or services which customers may not be interested in such as offering unwanted or spam emails regarding insurance, savings accounts, credit cards, investment schemes and new homeowner or help to buy schemes.

When working for a hypothetical private hire company, I can recall a time when a hypothetical customer insulted a worker at our firm. The worker was considering retaliating by cancelling their subscription.

This seemed to be ethically questionable since I have considered that this act would not be considered virtuous, the definition of virtue can be explored in Aristotle's concept of virtue.

Generally speaking, many of the theories on ethics would agree that it is wise to have an organisation which is based upon solid ethical rules.

These principles can be seen as a guideline for dealing with situations which cause doubt over an individual's ethical persuasion and also the organisation which they work for. They can also help an individual to reach a conclusion or consensus when faced with a problem related to ethics.

It is worthwhile mentioning concepts of rights, justice, integrity honesty, virtue and utilitarianism.

These concepts may all be considered when looking at ethics in an organization and decision-making surrounding ethics.

I will now merge two theories together in order to explain ethical reasoning and decision making within an organization. It may be considered that unethical decisions in business have a monetary value or cost, senior management lacking understanding of acts which may be considered questionable in an ethical sense, being able to understand the issue, considering the ethical issue from another perspective or opposing viewpoint, the steps which led to ethical mishap. Do you believe that the company will remain within the top 100, despite ethical problems occurring over a long period of time?

Robert E.Frederick, A companion to business Ethics it is stated *"Blanchard and Peale(1988)- recommend managers ask these questions before making a decision*

1 Is it legal?

2 Is it Balanced?

3 How will it make me feel about myself?

The market abuse regulation (MAR) was introduced in July 2016, it looks at providing increased market integrity, protection for investors and raising of capital for securities markets. Alexander Brink- Corporate Governance and Business Ethics states *"The shareholder (principal) employs the manager (agent) to act in his or her interests, namely so that the capital invested by the principal might bear as much interest as possible.*

MAR applies to financial instruments related for ones which are traded on a market regulated for which admission request for market trading has occurred.

Financial instruments which are related to multilateral trading platforms, which has been sent to MTF and when and admission request for an MTF has occurred.

Financial instruments which have been traded on an OTF.

Banks are regulated in order to prevent the failure of the banking system and banks as individuals and also to maintain confidence, integrity and trust in banks.

The laws and regulations in banking are mainly designed to act as controls for banks and to ensure the customers feel assured when doing business with their bank, when thinking of significant banking failure, it is possible to remember the case of Enron which was a catastrophic banking disaster.

The reason for banking failure can be attributed to inefficient decisions regarding investments, the bank being unable to keep pace because the customers withdraw money faster than the bank is prepared for, over time it leads to a deficit.

Essentially the whole point of regulation is ensuring that individuals feel that their money needs to stay in the bank because it benefits them as the customer. In this situation, there are regulations which help banks to make better management and investment decisions

The availability of complex financial options has led to an increase in the need to have a culture of security for assets, due to the abnormality created which led to an increase in a deviation of standard practice within the banking sector.

Some of large business have created a monopoly which has negatively affected customers.

Banking regulation in the UK consists of the treasury, FSA and bank of England, before the crisis, the regulators approach to banking was considered a light touch, however they did not wish to engage in heavier regulation since this may cause banks to seek other options.

In 2009, Lord Turner created a review into the crisis, he basically wanted better regulation for international banks, making sure that it has more co-ordination, able to deal with more assets, tighter regulations around liquidation etc.

Social responsibility for business was described by Milton Freedman as using resources to participate in activities which give increased profit, whilst sticking to the rules which are engaging in open and free competition with no fraud or deceptive elements there must also be an element of lawfulness and moral values since he mentions no deception or fraud and open / free competition.

Essentially Friedman is saying that management owes a duty to shareholders or owners, this may be interpreted as maximisation of ROI return on investment, or even return on investment with the promise of ethical practices.

Some may say that competition within the market which occurs freely between other businesses is a method of control, however this can grow unchecked and there is still the issue of corporate social responsibility (CSR) which may be infringed by this view.

Classical individualism has a far deeper level of ethics than what has been previously mentioned in Friedman's social responsibility.

There are several different versions of social responsibility, however the core concept is that the organisation has a responsibility which reaches further than the service or product which they give.

The concept is an ethical concept, it includes welfare, it provides a social outlook on the activities of a business or organization related to the concept of life improvement. It allows business to understand the social areas and the impact from a social standpoint.

There is an implied term around the obligation from a social stance, the concept may be considered normative and deals with the corporate behaviour and organisational policies which need to be implemented.

The social responsibility has several moral and ethical aspects including:

Businesses looking at the social aspect and the changes of this aspect in order to grow and thrive, businesses should adopt a more teleological or forecasted view on an individual's own interest in the business, and consider creating an improved environment through addressing and identifying social issues.

Businesses can gain a better reputation or face by appearing more socially aware and understanding the responsibilities of social aspects.

Regulations by the government become less of an issue if a business can accommodate the societal expectations, problems with social aspects can lead to unprofitable ventures, there is a moral expectation to eradicate social problems which a company or organisation has created.

A simple example of companies which have gone beyond their legal obligations would be harsh sales or bogus illegal companies, these companies essentially farm and prey upon young graduates or individuals new within the job market. They promise a competitive salary, company parties, benefits, bonuses/ commission.

However, the reality is that the individual is subjected to a brutal regime, which consists of hellish working hours, difficult working conditions, peer pressure, bullying, aggressive target driven culture and being treated almost as a corporate slave with no right to say no to extra working hours or difficult rules.

Legally these examples are bad since there should be a contract, which defines working hours, bonus structure, commission and there should also be clauses which prohibit bullying and the negative behaviour mentioned.

However, if Milton Friedman were a shareholder, one could argue that management owes a duty to its shareholders, it could be said that by imposing these harsh working conditions, the company is able to turn a profit and in turn the shareholders are able to obtain a ROI. Furthermore, looking at it from a legal standpoint the care owed may be considered a duty of care, similar to the case of Donoghue v Stevenson which ruled that a duty of care was owed to the individual who purchased the drink and found a snail inside.

There was also a case of whereby Volkswagen created a design which allowed them to skirt emissions control, which gave them a huge lead over their competitors and made them into one of the world leaders in car manufacturing. The story was that these cars were environmentally friendly when the opposite was actually true.

They rejected any form of ethical standard which led to some rather key oversights, the people responsible were aware of what was going on, the testing and various quality control test would have highlighted the issues to the individuals responsible for corporate social responsibility.

The processes, software, equipment and results were all on record, it is clear that Volkswagen deliberately hid the fact that this motor was not environmentally friendly, this leads back to the concept of virtue, integrity and even responsibility. These are all qualities which bankers should possess and which Volkswagen lacked in this particular instance, they were more interested in the maximisation of profit as opposed to environmental, factors, green energy and CSR.

It could however be argued that if Milton Friedman were a shareholder, it could be argued that Volkswagen have used resources and activities to increase profit,

An alternative theory to Friedman's view would deny social responsibility, it would ignore the duty which Friedman supposes owners owe to shareholders, a company could fail to justify some of the policies which it has which may be unethical or which may not agree with Milton Friedman's social responsibility or monetarist view which dictates that the performance of the economy is determined by changes in the supply of money, the health of the economy is related to these changes and changes in money or by a governing body.

The company may therefore adopt a different approach such as the Keynesian economics approach, this theory is related to output and inflation on total spending in the economy, Keynes essentially wanted lower tax rates and increased expenditure of the government. This would increase demand and change the tide of the recession.

If a company were to adopt this approach by John Maynard Keynes, they may for instance decide to adopt a policy which will help workers with the issue of income tax, this could mean implementing a commission structure or similar procedure, they would also look to increase demand. This could be done through the lowering of product price point or a smaller rotation of staff where necessary to reduce the cost of wages and maintain resources. In a banking sense rather than maximising ROI for shareholders as Friedman suggests, adopting a Keynesian approach you would look to maximise demand and you would control the rate of the return of investment in order to control the flow of money.

This could mean that you obtain more money over a longer period, which in turn would mean a larger amount for the investor, this can be considered unethical since you are temporarily ignoring the social responsibility.

Jacqueline Boakes questions whether leadership must not be democratic, her conclusion looks at the meaning of the relationship between both democracy and leadership, when looking at leadership, in regards to democracy it may be considered agnostic or neutral. There are certain types of leadership which have higher rates of compatibility than other types with regards to democracy.

This is due to the fact that we have reasons which are not associated with democracy, but which allow us to value it. Leadership is not compatible with democracy simply due to it's intrinsic nature, however some leadership styles support the way of democracy and its values.

A better argument for leadership with democracy is that there are attributes of leadership which are compatible with democracy, the true understanding of leadership will bind successfully with democracy.

The ethics of authentic leadership by Jessica Flannigan, states that authenticity is supported because of its positive moral attributes for leaders.

Inauthenticity may be likened with wrongful or deceitful acts such as deceiving an individual or acting as a hypocrite, the balance of decision for authenticity is based an emphasis on equal morals. Most leaders who are not authentic, usually do not give their followers the chance to agree to the plan of the leader and do not acknowledge these individuals as equal individuals with rights to equal morality.

However authentic leaders have loyalty which does not have illusions, and has occurred in a holistic and organic way with clear consent from their followers, leaders which are not authentic blame their followers and deny their equal moral rights by holding them to higher standards.

A leader who is not authentic may be altruistic in their intentions, a lack of authenticity is considered wrong because it lacks respect. It may still be justifiable, however in most cases it stems from mistaken morality permissible when it has not yet risen to the level of deception.

What makes a good leader?

Kant focuses on the intention behind the action as opposed to the action itself which one should be concerned with, he also mentions the point of universality, the idea of taking a concept which has a good intention and making that adopting that principle or maxim in every situation, such as in business a merchant who has good morals and a sense of honour, the actions which the merchant may have committed are bad and along with their intent. According to Kant they do not have good morals or honour.

Most importantly can the merchants honourable and good intentions be applied to every single merchant on a universal scale?

In Robert E.Frederick- A companion to business Ethics it is stated *"What does Kantian morality think our duties are? Kant distinguished between two kinds of duties (imperatives)"*

Social, political, ethical and ultimately metaphysical attributes can be given to the idea behind Plato's philosopher king as a style of leadership.

The ideas or paradigms around leadership and ethics are based on the origin and reasons for leadership, the questions surrounding leadership can only be answered by exploring the concepts of leadership and its connection with ethics.

Senior management and middle level employees may see themselves as another cog within the organisation and when adopting a leadership style, they may choose to shift responsibilities or adopt bad leadership habits.

Plato gives the example that the most suited leader is one who can inspire fear and achieve true leadership.

Robert E.Frederick, A companion to business Ethics states *"Kouzes (2010:xvii) set of conclusions based on survey responses for example are unconvincing and do not necessarily follow from the evidence he cites, for one thing the framework assumes that those asked know what qualities in a leader they most admire and are answering truthfully"*

The concept of Aristotle's virtue could be linked with ideas around individuals acting with integrity and in a professional manner, it is assumed that bankers would be highly professional and have a high sense of integrity, bankers should also be truthful with their customers and should not tell lies are also ethical assumptions.

Some of the technological developments include online banking- being able to transfer money for goods and services with a single click, the ability to identify and detect fraud has also been improved, we are now able to produce systems/ artificial intelligence which is able to detect fraud, this new system can detect fraud based on previous history and an algorithm is able to calculate whether an individual is committing fraud faster than a human can.

The development of autobots which provide advice and help services on banking websites, there is also more of a focus on using the website for guidance since many of the articles and services allow the user to access most of their banking features such as: applying for a mortgage, mortgage calculator, insurance, loans, ISA and Savings.

Other technological developments include telephone banking which allows an individual to access their banking services such transfers, direct debit and checking of balance by inputting their card number into the phone and going through security questions and inputting sensitive information.

The consideration for environmental factors relates to dealing with the issue related to climate change and the attempt to reduce our carbon foot print through the introduction of an economy which promotes low carbon usage.

The institute has stated its intention to move infrastructure and industries into a direction which supports the low carbon foot print and also creates a sustainable environment in the future economy.

It may be argued that another environmental factor which has recently affected banks is the recession which has occurred, what this recession means for business and banks is that they must find ways to lower their costs and overheads etc. Furthermore, this can be achieved by reducing the regulations on banks which allows them to hire due to the reduced cost from regulations.

Another factor which may be considered is the repayments associated with loans, due to the fact that loans are usually applied over a fixed period with rate of interest which varies based on payment, individuals will usually resort to faster alternatives to repay loans an increase in good/ services will allow them to repay the loans. The high amount of debt stimulates economic growth

A higher standard of housing services may be required by banks, banks will demand a higher ROI based on their highest form of lending which may be housing, as such the amount of money demanded is increased, the individuals with mortgages or rent which is repaid to the bank must therefore work more or attempt to increase the amount, they have borrowed in order to keep up and this in turn fuels the growth of the economy.

The issue is that all of the factors which lead to economic growth provide a direct increase in CO_2 emissions since it is an increase in the use of industry resources and manual labour which eventually involves the use of machines.

All of this threatens the ability to have a sustainable economy and environment, it is important for the future that the economy is sustainable since we are likely to face issues related to the environment such as pollution, climate change, global warming, food deprivation etc.

I will briefly touch on CSR, which is corporate social responsibility, a model which requires that an organisation is responsible socially for its produce and investors and stakeholders. This is an issue which most businesses are considering, however it should be considered more in order to obtain a sustainable economic environment.

There is a large selection of different types of banks ranging from banks which provide a retail purpose or there are banks which provide wholesale services.

The argument for banks having a moral obligation towards the environment one of the ideas which would support this argument is the idea of corporate social responsibility- this theory states companies should be aware of their responsibility to appear as organisations which acknowledge and address their shortcomings and also look to always have socials awareness and political understanding of their company's position and undertakings.

This ideal may be closely linked in with ideas such as: having green energy and considering the effect of waste and business practices on the environment, a simple example would be a bank which was still using a paper system for their database storage this would not be considered environmentally friendly and it would also not align with CSR.

Reordering responsibilities will lead to an increase or a reshuffling of moral obligations, it now possible for tasks which were previously carried out as s single process to now be shared processes.

We must also consider environmental sustainability, how sustainable is the current economic situation and our environment. This question is not easy to answer since the economy is affected by lending from consumers and public spending.

The more lending and borrow which occurs the more economic growth which occurs, if individuals borrow a large amount of money, they must conversely work more in order to pay this back or borrow more. Both of these actions have a positive effect on economy and industry.

For instance, going back in history a kingdom from the Middle Ages was able make advancements when they treasury or coffers were full from collecting taxes and they were able to fund research or invest some money in a large-scale project or developing a simple bridge.

However considering the question on morality to the environment when banking, it should be considered how they have the moral obligation or how they do not have the obligation.

It may be considered tacit knowledge to say that banks have a moral obligation to their employees and customers since there is a contract, legal or law principles and the ethical theorists who seem to agree with this view for instance Milton Friedman.

However, the environment may refer to several factors for instance would environment refer to issues which affect our ecosystem such as global warming, climate change, CO_2 emissions, fossil fuels, resources becoming scarcer etc. or does this refer to the economic. environment such as: recession which occurred recently, hyperinflation in the Weimar republic occurring between 1921 to 1923, caused employment difficulty, a rise in gas/ fuel prices or stock market, increase in alternatives this includes: alternative goods such as silver, alternative investments etc.

The banks have a moral obligation to the customer and the customers are affected by their environment, therefore, it may be considered that banks have a moral obligation to the environment indirectly. This would mean that banks should adopt policies which consider climate change, damages to the environment, reduction in resources.

This raises another issue since if banks consider the environment as a priority from moral obligation, how will they be able to obtain efficiency and large profits? It has been stated that economic growth stems from increased borrowing, working, spending, buying of estates, mortgages and investment.

All of these factors increase CO2 emissions, global warming, as well as spending resources and are generally bad for the environment. A graph will show the direct correlation between increased CO2, increased industrial work, banking and economic growth.

Is there a way for banks to be green while maintain profit and stability? Can they uphold the moral obligation and still be loyal to customers and profit maximisation.

Bibliography

Robert E.Frederick- A companion to business Ethics(1999) ISBN 1-4051-0102-4

Jacqueline Boaks & Michael P Levine-Leadership & Ethics (2015) ISBN 978-1-350-02828-9

R.G Frey and Christopher Heath Wellman- A companion to Applied Ethics (2003)

Alexander Brink- Corporate Governance and Business Ethics (2011)

The Chartered Banker Code of Professional Conduct January (2016) viewed on 26 December 2019 available from: http://www.cbpsb.org/

Justine Rogers, Dimity Kingsford Smith and John Chellew -Banking and the Limits of Professionalism (2017) viewed on 26 December 2019 available from http://www.unswlawjournal.unsw.edu.au/article/banking-and-the-limits-of-professionalism/

ICAEW Jim Baxter,James Dempsey,Chris Megone et al - Real Integrity Practical Solutions For Organisations Seeking To Encourage Integrity (2012) viewed 26 December 2019 available from http://www.unswlawjournal.unsw.edu.au/article/the-large-professional-service-firm-a-new-force-in-the-regulative-bargain/

Luigi Wegewege and Michael C. Thomsett, The Digital Banking revolution- How fintech companies are transforming the retail banking industry through financial innovation 3rd Edition (2019)

Linda K. Trevino, Katherine A. Nelson Managing Business Ethics- straight talk about how to do it right 6th edition (2014)

Linda K. Trevino, Katherine A. Nelson Managing Business Ethics- straight talk about how to do it right 5th edition (2010)

www.ingramcontent.com/pod-product-compliance
Lightning Source LLC
Chambersburg PA
CBHW071443210326
41597CB00020B/3917